4/9/18

Dear Sis. Ernestine,

You are such a sweet
and loving jewel in the
Body of Christ! I am so
glad to know you. May
God continue to meet your
every need, spirit, soul and
body, in Jesus' Name.
Love, Stephanie Howard

TABLE OF CONTENTS

FOREWORDS

Stephanie Howard is beautiful from the depths of her soul to the radiance that shows throughout her countenance. She is an author, minister and poet. She is a nurturer of the heart, mind and soul. She is inspirational and motivational both in speech and the written word. I like to call this awesome woman of God a word wizard, not just because she knows how to weave her words into a lovely tapestry of poetic soundness and truths, but because her words resound from her heart and echo throughout your senses.

Although this book's backdrop and references are biblical and tells the story of Prophet Elijah's temptation to give up, the story depicts the struggles that we all have encountered on a daily basis. We have all been in the "CAVE". This book speaks of "coming out" of the darkness of despair and fear into the marvelous light of victory. Journey with her as she walks you through step by step.

    — *Rev. Caprice D. Nesbit-Turane, MSW*
       Daughters of Zion International Ministries,
       Inc., Warriors for Christ
       Pastor/Founder

The journey of every Christian is uniquely different but, there are some similarities. God calls all of us to a place of Faith and Trust in Him. In spite of numerous social obstacles, and demonic attacks, our own willingness to be honest with ourselves and true to God's call on our lives, self-transparency is critical.

In this book, Stephanie Howard has opened up the challenges and the importance of God's call on your life from an early age, and offers a fresh stream of understanding the heart of God as it relates to His children. I have been blessed by this book, it will challenge your Spiritual maturity. Howard suggests to us that spiritual maturity is measured by the change produced by the presence of God and His word in our lives.

As you read this book, be open to the power of God as it jumps off the pages and transforms your life as it has done for Howard, as she pens her experience with God so openly. I am impressed by Stephanie and the great presence of God that surrounds her. She not only walks in extraordinary miracles, signs and wonders, but she also has been supernaturally equipped by God to make disciples and move them to a place of knowing God supernaturally for themselves, bringing a freshness to their lives.

— *Rev. Dr. Keith Hayward, Pastor*
Bethel A.M.E. Church, Copiague, New York

Using the backdrop of the familiar-to-most story of Elijah, his meeting with the prophets of Baal, and his confrontation with Jezebel, Stephanie shares profound treasures of truth that a casual reader of the Scripture might easily miss but needs to add to his life.

>   – *Linda Stubblefield, Editor and Writer*
>   *Affordable Christian Editing*

I am a free spirit, having gone through many different religious cultures in my 80 years. When I was reading this book as a proofreader, I found that it grabbed hold of me in a deeply spiritual way. The author's matter-of-fact faith was shining throughout the whole book. It felt as if she led me by the hand out of my own cave – that I hadn't realized I was in! I want my children and grandchildren to read this important book.

>   – *Connie MacNamee, Proofreader and*
>   *Jazz Singer*

PREFACE

The storms of life had packed a one-two punch and a couple of kicks, leaving me in a position where there was no quick fix, no pat answer, no one person or formula that could put whipped cream and a cherry on top of my circumstances. My daughter, my only child was gone, in an instant. There were circumstances leading up to that point, and circumstances following, that shook me to my very core. I instantly became a mom again at the birth of my granddaughter, which shows that it is indeed true, that inside the clouds is a silver lining.

Waking up in the mornings, greeted by simultaneous joy and sorrow, the pain and emptiness in my gut let me know it had not been a troublesome dream, this was a new reality that I would learn to live with and walk through daily. The comforting part about it was that what my faith had taught proved to be true, and was a rock I could stand on when the ground threatened to give way: "The steadfast love of the Lord never ceases, His mercies never come to an end. They are new every morning. Great is Thy faithfulness."

Fast forward several years to the 'conception' of this book. My 'pregnancy' began with a workshop two years ago at my church's Women's Retreat. I was assigned the task of conducting a one-hour workshop for about twenty women age 65 and over. Prayerfully I came up with the theme and title "Come Out of the Cave, You're Not Done Yet." At the end of the day, the material was still stirring in me, and I heard inside "This should be a book." I thought, yes, that would be a nice idea, and went on with living. The nudge came back again and again, more frequently and insistently.

Why hadn't I acted on it more immediately? Because I wrestled within with the 'who, me?' of actually 'parenting' this book. I wondered if the dormancy of my womb, representing creativity, was capable of sustaining this new life. Then one day God just began to pour out the chapter titles as I grabbed my pen and hurriedly tried to keep pace with the divine dictation I was receiving! And so the seed began to germinate and I began to write.

This book, the 'fetus,' began to grow, with God sometimes stirring me with 'cravings' in the midnight hours with a thought or a concept to flesh out later, or the 'morning sickness' of wondering if I'd be a good mother to this baby, or the 'nesting' of hopes I'd be prepared to raise and nurture it properly. But guess what, no matter how I felt, that baby was still coming!

I would pick the manuscript up, and put it down. After a season of having put it down, I got a 'kick', when on July 4, 2017, during my time of morning prayer, Holy Spirit spoke to me and said *"If you're not going to finish the book, I may as well bring you home."* WHAT???!!! I then realized that this was not just my little project, but I was carrying a child of great purpose. So, guess what I did on the 4th of July? WRITE!!!

On one level, this book was born out of a workshop. On a deeper level, this book was born on top of a foundation laid from my own cave experience and the events surrounding it. As God poured into me what He wanted said, and related it to the story of Elijah, I then saw, on paper, the steps He had used in my very own trials. What I experienced was by divine, day-in, day-out relationship with the Most High, with the gamut of raw emotions, sprinkled with times of love, hope, faith, joy, laughter, and strength, with the help of those He sent along the way as vessels to assist. The Lord is yet guiding me into my future, through what has been revealed to me in these pages.

If you are reading this book, chances are you are one whom God urgently wanted to reach out and touch. Or perhaps He wants you to bring it to the attention of someone else who may be in need.

So, with that in mind, I humbly present to you my newborn baby, my first book, breathed through me from the breath of God:

COME OUT OF THE CAVE
You're Not Done Yet!

I pray that the purpose of this child will be realized in your life, and that each word will accomplish what it was designed by God to accomplish. May your journey be blessed.

Stephanie

ACKNOWLEDGMENTS

My heartfelt gratitude for helping make this project a reality:

God:

For keeping me alive and for impregnating this concept within me.

Family Encouragers:

Destiny, for all your love and support.

My parents Valerie & Charles Crawford for believing.

My Sistah/Cousins, Rev. Janice Tudy-Jackson and
Rev. Mercedes Tudy-Hamilton, for your love, prayer and support.

Project Contributors:

Rev. Caprice Nesbit-Turane and Rev. Dr. Keith Hayward for your
leadership and support, and for your amazing Forewords. I'm humbled.

McLendon Bowden for catching the vision with your anointed
and breathtaking cover artwork.

The "MacNanimous" Connie MacNamee, for giving of your
time and talent towards the first proofreading and edit, and
for your amazing feedback.

Linda Stubblefield of Affordable Christian Editing for your editing,
prayers and encouragement.

Author Daphne Beard for being my forerunner and for dropping
wisdom seeds on the path before me.

*ALL WHO SPOKE WORDS OF PRAYER, ENCOURAGEMENT, WISDOM
AND EXHORTATION IN DUE SEASON.*

♥ *Thank you, Bless you, Love you!* ♥

INTRODUCTION

The storm. Storms come to every person's life. They are inevitable.

Sometimes the storm is gracious enough to give you advanced warning that it's coming so you're prepared. You can see the foreboding clouds in the distance. The meteorologist warns you it's on the horizon, giving you ample time to buy needed home supplies and groceries, and to make sure your movie account is paid up to date so you can comfortably ride out the storm.

Some storms come out of nowhere. You're literally blindsided. The force of the winds, the velocity, and the rage of the storm are more than you can bear, far exceeding your most well-conceived plans and stocked-up resources.

The place of security on which you stood yesterday is uprooted and eroded; tomorrow seems very distant and full of uncertainty, and your challenge for today is catching your next breath.

This is the point when you may find yourself running for shelter…running for your very life. And in your flight for safety, you find the C.A.V.E.—COVERING AGAINST THE VERY EXTREME.

Nobody will find you there. It's dark, hidden, off the beaten path. This place of refuge may not be very comfortable, but it's safe. You light a candle, put some rocks together for a pillow—a place to lay your head. It's lonely, but you find companionship in the crawling spider, the occasional bat that flies by, or the rodent that scampers across the ground. It's cold and damp, but you cover up and say, *"This is temporary—just a place to catch my breath, to figure things out, to get my bearings…"*

But the moments become days, the days become months, and the months become years. The cave becomes home; the hideout becomes a dwelling place. All concept of time is lost in the cave. Yesterday, which becomes "the good old days," has now become the highlight, the apex of your life, as you see it from the cave.

The dreams, the goals, the plans and the purpose for tomorrow are now only a fast-extinguishing flicker, uprooted and washed away by the storm.

The cave has been your place of survival, of making do, of existing, of staying afloat, of biding your time, until...

The darkness, the dimness and the dampness of the cave begin to play tricks on your mind. You no longer feel that you can make it to the light of day. You become very self-focused, self-existent, and the thought of what's happening outside of the cave in the real world with other people is too much to think about. After all, you have your own problems just trying to make it yourself!

Is this *you*?

As you have read this description, has your storm come to mind? Do you remember the day and the hour when everything changed in your life? Can you state the location of your cave? Are you dwelling there now?

After a season of deep personal tragedy, I took refuge and then residence in my own personal cave…until I heard the same message I have been unctioned to share with you:

COME OUT OF THE CAVE

You're Not Done Yet!

There was a man named Elijah in biblical scripture, who was a person of great strength, hope, purpose, and promise. In anguish of soul, in response to a "storm" in his life, he retreated into a cave. In the darkness and bleakness of his cave and in the frailty of his humanness, he could not see even a flicker of hope. However, when he heard and embraced the message to come out of that cave, that his journey was not yet complete, that his finest hours were not behind him but still ahead of him, through no strength of his own, he took the first step…and the rest is history.

Have the storms of life caused you to find yourself in a cave-like experience? Join me on a journey, with you as the main character and Elijah's story as the backdrop, that will provide precious keys to walking out of that cave, towards and through fulfillment of purpose.

This book is not about me, though the path has and is affecting me greatly. Instead, this book is personalized with you in mind. If you find that the jacket fits, please, put it on. If the shoe fits, wear it. If it adds to your journey, you're welcomed to receive it as a gift from God to you.

Are you ready to consider taking that first step? Come on, let's go. Turn the page.

1

ON THE HEELS OF VICTORY

1 KINGS 18

[36]At the usual time for offering the evening sacrifice, Elijah the prophet walked up to the altar and prayed, "O Lord God of Abraham, Isaac, and Jacob, prove today that you are God in Israel and that I am your servant. Prove that I have done all this at your command. [37]O Lord, answer me! Answer me so these people will know that you, O Lord, are God and that you have brought them back to yourself."

[38]Immediately the fire of the Lord flashed down from heaven and burned up the young bull, the wood, the stones, and the dust. It even licked up all the water in the trench! [39]And when all the people saw it, they fell face down on the ground and cried out, "The Lord —He is God! Yes, the Lord is God!"

Have you ever had that day when it seemed like everything was in alignment? There was a flow, a charge, an energy…it seemed as if the reason for your very existence was coming to fruition. You experienced a victory that was downright miraculous.

As you reflect on the happenings of the day, you stand, holding your trophy of victory. The sun is beaming down on you, your eyes are filled with tears of joy, your heart is overwhelmed with awe and wonder, and you're proud. You're proud of you and proud of God. Is this where you attach the phrase: "And they lived happily ever after?"

Surely you've reached the culmination of life, the peak of goodness. Surely your hard work has paid off, and you can now live off the rewards of your labors from this time forth, even for evermore!

Wouldn't it be grand if life were always like that? Instead, situations and circumstances may arise, much like a storm, that were totally unexpected, and in your opinion, are even uncalled for.

Although we'd like to think that our lives will be an ever-ascending climb up the ladder of success, life shows us that even as in the best of fairy tales, our journey consists of twists and turns, peaks and valleys, fair weather and storms, and yes, even some "caves."

Perhaps you may feel that just when you thought the proverbial puzzle pieces of life had come together perfectly, in came the upheaval of the storm.

For this book, a storm is not necessarily a meteorological event, though it may be. My definition of a **storm** is:

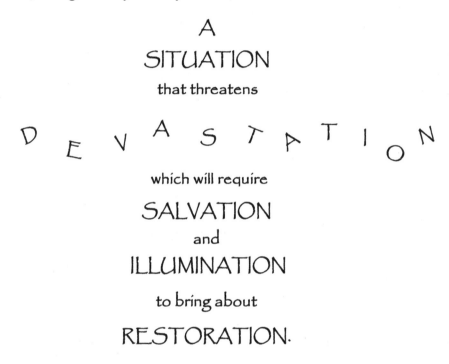

A
SITUATION
that threatens

D E V A S T A T I O N
which will require
SALVATION
and
ILLUMINATION
to bring about
RESTORATION.

Elijah the Prophet helped to facilitate and experience a monumental and miraculous occurrence that was indeed victorious. The outcome was just as he had hoped. It was one of those events that you could stick a pin in as a life marker, an event that would be remembered and talked about for years, even generations to come.

Let me give you the backstory. There was an *inauguration*.

1 KINGS 16

29 Ahab son of Omri began to rule over Israel in the thirty-eighth year of King Asa's reign in Judah. He reigned in Samaria twenty-two years. 30 But Ahab son of Omri did what was evil in the Lord's sight, even more than any of the kings before him. 31 And as though it were not enough to follow the sinful example of Jeroboam, he married Jezebel, the daughter of King Ethbaal of the Sidonians, and he began to bow down in worship of Baal. 32 First Ahab built a temple and an altar for Baal in Samaria. 33 Then he set up an Asherah pole. He did more to provoke the anger of the Lord, the God of Israel, than any of the other kings of Israel before him.

Elijah emerged, apparently on a mission under *authorization* by God, and made a *declaration*.

1 KINGS 17

1Now Elijah, who was from Tishbe in Gilead, told King Ahab, "As surely as the LORD, the God of Israel, lives—the God I serve—there will be no dew or rain during the next few years until I give the word!"

Just as Elijah declared, there was indeed no rainfall, and this severely impacted the region. Three years later, as instructed by God, Elijah made a ***proclamation***.

In her efforts to remove the Lord's influence on the region, Queen Jezebel was intent on ***annihilation*** of the Lord's prophets.

Then came the ***accusation*** by King Ahab that Elijah was the source of their problems.

Which led to the *demonstration* that resulted in the *realization* that the Lord is God.

[19] Now summon all Israel to join me at Mount Carmel, along with the 450 prophets of Baal and the 400 prophets of Asherah who are supported by Jezebel."

[20] So Ahab summoned all the people of Israel and the prophets to Mount Carmel. [21] Then Elijah stood in front of them and said, "How much longer will you waver, hobbling between two opinions? If the Lord is God, follow him! But if Baal is God, then follow him!" But the people were completely silent.

[36] At the usual time for offering the evening sacrifice, Elijah the prophet walked up to the altar and prayed, "O Lord God of Abraham, Isaac, and Jacob, prove today that you are God in Israel and that I am your servant. Prove that I have done all this at your command. [37] O Lord, answer me! Answer me so these people will know that you, O Lord, are God and that you have brought them back to yourself."

[38] Immediately the fire of the Lord flashed down from heaven and burned up the young bull, the wood, the stones, and the dust. It even licked up all the water in the trench! [39] And when all the people saw it, they fell face down on the ground and cried out, "The Lord —He is God! Yes, the Lord is God!"

Accusation

Elijah was accused of being a troublemaker for doing what he was called and sent to do – to shake and to shift the atmosphere.

Carrying out purpose, resulting in good, positive changes in our own lives and the lives of others, may sometimes incite a less-than-favorable response from the people around us. While God may be rejoicing over your victories, others for whatever reason may not share the same sentiments.

When faced with a destructive storm, you may ask yourself the question: *"What did I do wrong?"* But are you to blame?

Others may be more than happy to respond with a long list of your imperfections, perhaps even going so far as to cite you as the reason for the storm.

Instead of asking *"What did I do wrong,"* perhaps the question should be: *"What did I do right?"*

"What did I do to anger the forces of wrong? What light was shone into dark places?"

Washed Up, But Not Washed Out

1 KINGS 18

33bThen he said, "Fill four large jars with water, and pour the water over the offering and the wood."

34After they had done this, he said, "Do the same thing again!" And when they were finished, he said, "Now do it a third time!" So they did as he said, 35and the water ran around the altar and even filled the trench.

36At the usual time for offering the evening sacrifice, Elijah the prophet walked up to the altar and prayed, "O Lord God of Abraham, Isaac, and Jacob, prove today that you are God in Israel and that I am your servant. Prove that I have done all this at your command. 37O Lord, answer me! Answer me so these people will know that you, O Lord, are God and that you have brought them back to yourself."

38Immediately the fire of the Lord flashed down from heaven and burned up the young bull, the wood, the stones, and the dust. **It even licked up all the water in the trench!** 39And when all the people saw it, they fell face down on the ground and cried out, "The Lord —He is God! Yes, the Lord is God!"

In this scripture, instruction is given to repeatedly pour water on something that is expected to catch on fire. Pour water all over the sacrifice. Sometimes the storm will dump water all over *you*! Through the eyes of others, your circumstances may make you seem 'all washed up'. They may say, *"There's no way*

13

anything good can be done through you! It's impossible! You're drenched, saturated, incombustible... Ain't no way!"

God is still able to manifest Himself in and through you. Don't give up hope! My friend, you're exactly the one who God would choose to use when the fire falls. Why? So He will receive all the glory. He uses the foolish things to confound the wise. In Elijah's demonstration, when all the people saw the fire, they fell on their faces and said, "The Lord He is God, the Lord He is God!"

Who's to Blame?

Perhaps it's a backlash.

Backlash is defined as "a strong, adverse or violent reaction; a sudden, forceful backward movement; recoil." A backlash is what happens when our enemy hits back at us immediately after he's experienced a setback.

A backlash can deliver a blow with the capacity to knock you off your feet, for an instant. The backlash may cause you to think momentarily, *"Maybe I shouldn't have done that."*

Although the backlash can be uncomfortable, to say the least, its discomfort is not to be compared to the pain of *not* doing what you are called and created to be and do.

Where is God in this backlash? Whenever there is chaos, revelation is on the way. Look for it.

What you see going on around you and what you have experienced has nothing to do with God's loving you. He still does.

God is not the cause for everything. Man has free will and free choice. We are living in a land and a time when the ugliness would mar the very beauty designed by God.

We often hear about God's getting both the blame and the credit for all kinds of things. "God caused…" "God took…" "An act of God." We know the event is bigger than man, but that does not mean it was caused by God.

More is going on around us than is seen by the naked eye. Ephesians 6:12 says, *"For we are not fighting against flesh-and-blood enemies, but against evil rulers and authorities of the unseen world, against mighty powers in this dark world, and against evil spirits in the heavenly places."*

Preparation for the Storm

When we hear of an impending natural storm, we may choose to board up our windows and any openings of the house, to protect our homes and families as best we can. Just as we would do in a natural storm, this would be a good time to shore up our spiritual house, by doing a spiritual self-evaluation. The Bible says that the spirit of man is the candlestick of the Lord. Using the flashlight of the Spirit and the compass of His Word, guided by His Spirit, we cover the openings, windows and doorways that may be open, accessible or vulnerable in the storm, strengthening the weakest links in our lives and our family. What are we covering them with? God made a way out of no way through the very powerful blood of Jesus.

Running Into the Storm

1 KINGS 18

⁴¹Then Elijah said to Ahab, "Go get something to eat and drink, for I hear a mighty rainstorm coming!"

⁴²So Ahab went to eat and drink. But Elijah climbed to the top of Mount Carmel and bowed low to the ground and prayed with his face between his knees.

⁴³Then he said to his servant, "Go and look out toward the sea."

The servant went and looked, then returned to Elijah and said, "I didn't see anything."

Seven times Elijah told him to go and look. ⁴⁴Finally the seventh time, his servant told him, "I saw a little cloud about the size of a man's hand rising from the sea."

Then Elijah shouted, "Hurry to Ahab and tell him, 'Climb into your chariot and go back home. If you don't hurry, the rain will stop you!'"

⁴⁵And soon the sky was black with clouds. A heavy wind brought a terrific rainstorm, and Ahab left quickly for Jezreel. ⁴⁶Then the Lord gave special strength to Elijah. He tucked his cloak into his belt and ran ahead of Ahab's chariot all the way to the entrance of Jezreel.

There was a heavy wind which brought a terrific rainstorm. Was this the storm Elijah was facing? No, this was a welcome weather condition, a fulfillment of Elijah's declaration that it would not rain again until *he* said so. After the hearts of the people were turned, the rain returned. This was a restoration and replenishing of what had been lost in the season of drought, brought on by rebellion.

However, there was an ominous storm brewing, and Elijah was about to run straight into it, for Jezreel housed the palace of King Ahab and Queen Jezebel.

On the heels of victory, Elijah was running right into the face of the threat…

2

THE THREAT

1 KINGS 19

²So Jezebel sent this message to Elijah: "May the gods strike me and even kill me if by this time tomorrow I have not killed you just as you killed them."

Surely you knew your actions would anger someone. But under obedience to the hand and the guidance of God, you were compelled to carry out what you were guided to accomplish— maybe even were born to accomplish. *"...Nevertheless, not my will, but thine, be done."* (Luke 22:42).

At the time, we are so consumed with purpose that there really is no other way. We are crossing over to the other side!

Then through the natural ear, you hear the sound of the threat. Elijah was a strong man who had just performed great and marvelous feats in concert with God, and yet the voicing of the threat by this one woman stopped him dead in his tracks. Fear gripped his body.

Hearing that threat had the power to shift Elijah's focus from the power of God to the source of the threat. The prophet knew he was dealing with a person consumed with evil intent. Just hearing the sound and knowing the heart and mind behind the voice sent chills and stopped him in his tracks. His physical senses kicked in and began to overtake him.

You may ask how the switch could be flipped so quickly and easily to cause Elijah to come screeching to a halt. The human body has been designed with a built-in response to fear. The sound of Jezebel's threat became amplified, magnified, very present, and perhaps sent a shockwave through his system.

According to scientific research on the physical effects of fear, the following is a list of reactions and symptoms one may experience:

- Increased heart rate and blood flow to the muscles so a person can run faster
- Fight or flight survival mechanism designed to keep one safe signals the body to prepare for danger

- Increased flow of hormones to the amygdala, an area of brain to help one focus on the present danger and store it in their memory

- As certain brain pathways short-circuit in the face of fear, more rational processing paths are ramped up

- Perception of events is changed to negative and stored that way

- All of the details surrounding sights, sounds, odors, the time of day, and the weather type can become durable, yet sometimes are fragmented memories that can become stimuli and trigger fear and PTSD

- Constant fear and anxiety impair health, interrupt brain processes and make one act out

- In one's susceptibility to intense emotions, they become unable to act appropriately.

Did one woman's threat really instill that kind of fear when hundreds of prophets of Baal could not?

Scientific research indicates that it's as though the brain has been hijacked at the onset of fear. It's not the person; it's the evil behind the person who has generated the fear. The results

21

of the storm—that traumatic event—have become like a recording, forming grooves that, when triggered, just like a scratched record, play over and over again.

Change the Record

According to scientific research, the process of **overcoming** a fear memory is known as "fear extinction." Fear extinction involves **creating** a new response to the fear-causing stimulus, **retraining** the amygdala in the brain by making positive associations, thus **rewriting** the fear response.

If we find the same fear recording is playing over and over again, we can take the authority to cut it off. Change the record! It's not God's will for us to be ensnared in this place. Scripture says, *"Faith comes by hearing, and hearing by the Word of God."* (Romans 10:17) *"For God has not given us the spirit of fear; but of power, and of love, and of a sound mind."* (2 Timothy 1:7) By hearing and submitting to the new recording of God's Word, the old response can be rewritten.

New sound, new vision…

3

LOOK INTO THE MIRROR; WHAT DO YOU SEE?

1 KINGS 19

³Elijah was afraid and fled for his life.

CEO, Associate, Manager, Director, Dr., Esq., Reverend, Tom's wife, Donna's husband, Simone's mom, Mr. Halloway's son, Mrs. Brown's daughter, Chief, Coach, Armor bearer, Deacon.

You have earned that title or maybe another. You studied hard year after year, endured and overcame trial after trial, with the scars to prove it. You have a wall full of certificates, diplomas proudly mounted, trophies displayed in the case, and even newspaper clippings to show your victories. You have honor in the marketplace. You have won the respect of your peers. You've climbed the corporate ladder. What you say goes.

You look in the mirror and smile with a sense of satisfaction. *"I am kind, I am smart, I am important! I've found the formula. There's nowhere but up from here!"*

Before the storm.

Suddenly and without warning, the storm hits. The unexpected visits life and suddenly, what you heard, stood for, spent years cultivating, planning and executing, is gone.

And you don't know what to do.

Circumstances happen and, depending on the severity, may have the capacity to knock you off your feet, shake you to your very core, and completely shift the dynamic of your very identity.

Look into the mirror. NOW what do you see?

Perhaps you've been widowed, orphaned, downsized, empty-nested, divorced, financially challenged, diagnosed with a chronic illness, served with repossession papers... Not that happily-ever-after you planned for?

Who are you now? After the storm?

Elijah the prophet was well-known, well-respected, feared, and full of power. He had only recently declared no rain would fall again until he said so, and he had victoriously engaged hundreds in the challenge to prove his God was the true God. After he had announced that it would now rain again, during a terrific rainstorm with the assistance of the Lord's mighty hand, he outran the king's chariot.

Before the storm—before the threat—he was confident and had the track record to prove it.

After the storm, Elijah lost confidence in Whose he was. His circumstances told him he was a has-been, that he was no match for this evil foe, that he was washed up.

Has who you see in the mirror been changed by your circumstances?

25

Do you reminisce about the good old days, what used to be? Are your best days behind you?

Has the storm created a dividing line between your "before" and your "after"?

Where there was once muscle and stamina, is there now only weakness and weariness? Where there was once courage, is there now fear? Where there was once confidence, is there now insecurity?

Has the fire in your eyes become a flicker? Has your get-up-and-go gotten up and gone?

Does what happened on the outside really have the power to change who you are on the inside?

I know what they say: "This joy I have the world didn't give it, and the world can't take it away." Have you lost your joy?

Is this storm so overwhelming that you feel like you must go somewhere and hide? Elijah did exactly that...

4

THE HIDING PLACE

Gotta get away and breathe…get away from the friends, the people looking up to you, the people expecting to draw from you…

You've been the source of strength for others; you've prided yourself on being the go-to person, the one with the answers, the one with the divine hookup. Now your divine connection feels fuzzy. You hear only static on the line.

I don't understand why. Is my solid Rock solid enough to hold me? I just want to get away, to process this pain. It's overwhelming.

Sometimes you have to just get away from the routine for a little while. Take a retreat.

But we are never to run away from God. It's best to run toward Him. Draw close to Him and He will draw close to you!

In the song "I Love the Lord", the songwriter declares, "Long as I live, when troubles rise, I'll hasten to His throne."

You're welcome at the throne, just as you are. If your heart is drawing you, don't worry about what shape you're in; just go!

Anguish of Soul

1 KINGS 19

⁴Then he went on alone into the wilderness, traveling all day. He sat down under a solitary broom tree and prayed that he might die. "I have had enough, Lord," he said. "Take my life, for I am no better than my ancestors who have already died."

Elijah wanted to get far, far away from everyone, everything, into an isolated place. A wilderness, if you would.

He sat down under a solitary broom tree. Everything about him was lonely, solitary, isolated, depressed.

28

Elijah decided to pray. He prayed what was on his heart and mind. He could not see a way out and, based on that inability, based on his weariness, hopelessness and despair of the moment, he asked God to end his life.

There is hope for tomorrow, even when the windshield wipers of our soul don't move fast enough to dry the tears from our eyes.

Hope for tomorrow comes with divine assistance. We cannot do it on our own. Don't give up on God.

LUKE 4

[18]"The Spirit of the Lord is upon me,
for he has anointed me to bring Good News to the poor.
He has sent me to proclaim that captives will be released,
that the blind will see, that the oppressed will be set free,
[19]and that the time of the Lord's favor has come."

Testimony

During rush hour, I stood sobbing on track three of the busy railroad hub in Queens, New York. My tears were blinding and came from a heart so shattered that I could no longer find enough Band-Aids to patch. I was 19-years-old, and the boyfriend I thought I couldn't live without had gone into a relationship with someone else. In my 19-year-old mind, with a history of feeling dejected by the circumstances of life, I was devastated with no hope for tomorrow.

I was familiar with the schedule and knew that a non-stop express train would come barreling through, and even now, the train was coming up the track. I prepared to jump, thinking this act would end my pain. As I watched the headlights of the train fast approaching the station, I suddenly heard a very calming male voice behind me say, "It can't be that bad."

As I turned towards the voice, to see who was speaking to me, the train barreled through the station and passed me by. The gentleman was wearing a tan-colored trench coat and had the most gentle eyes I'd ever seen. He handed me a tissue. In the moment that it took to dry my eyes, I looked again, and he was gone. I looked up and down the platform, and he was nowhere in sight...

I knew I had been visited by an angel.

God cares. Don't give up. Wait for His help.

Provision for the Weary Soul

1 Kings 19

⁵Then he lay down and slept under the broom tree. But as he was sleeping, an angel touched him and told him, "Get up and eat!" ⁶He looked around and there beside his head was some bread baked on hot stones and a jar of water! So he ate and drank and lay down again.

⁷Then the angel of the Lord came again and touched him and said, "Get up and eat some more, or the journey ahead will be too much for you."

⁸So he got up and ate and drank, and the food gave him enough strength to travel forty days and forty nights to Mount Sinai, the mountain of God. ⁹There he came to a cave, where he spent the night.

All Elijah could do in his state of fear and weariness was fall asleep. The Bible says that he was awakened by an angel who told him to "Get up and eat!" Angelic help is real, my friend; I am a witness! Already prepared for Elijah was baked bread and a jar of water. So he ate and went back to sleep.

Sometimes you may only have enough strength to eat and sleep. Receive the help God is providing and rest in His arms. Allow Him to nurse you through this place and season.

*Then the angel of the L*ORD *came again...and said, "Get up and eat some more, or the journey ahead will be too much for you." So he got up and ate and drank, and the food gave him enough strength to travel forty days and forty nights to Mount Sinai, the mountain of God.*

It took all that to get Elijah into the presence of God, the mountain of God, the elevated place where he could grieve and rest and rise above the situation, for a little while. A sanctuary, if you will.

There in the mountain of God, Elijah came to a cave where he decided to spend *the night*...

5
The Extended Stay—Setting Up Shop

1 Kings 19

⁸So he got up and ate and drank, and the food gave him enough strength to travel forty days and forty nights to Mount Sinai, the mountain of God. ⁹There he came to a cave, where he spent the night.

Surely, in the mountain of God must be all of the provision we could possibly want or need. That mountain must be a place where we can finally inhale and exhale. There we can take a breather, and get our head together. In the mountain, we can rest...be rejuvenated...revived...restored.

In the mountain of God, Elijah found a cave...a place he felt safe—where no one could find him.

No doubt, that cave was dark, damp, desolate. There was probably a rock on which he could rest his head. There was probably a spider web, a rodent, or even a bat flying by. As uncomfortable as it was, Elijah sought out that cave as his resting place…for the night…

How many of us have turned in at the cave—supposedly for a night, which turned into two nights, three nights, then a week, a month, a year, or more…

The uncomfortable became not so bad…our eyes adjusted to the darkness. We became friends with the spiders and affectionately made the rodent our household pet and companion. We hung "curtains" on the wall and adjusted to the pillow of stone beneath our head. We felt a sense of safety and security.

We were "doing what we had to do"—accepting less-than-desirable employment, living in less than optimal conditions, resigning ourselves that this is how it will have to be, until the kids are grown, until we retire, until we die…

We couldn't see our way clear to leave, sure that the threat was still looming large outside of the cave, right around the corner.

Living in a constant state of alert has taken its toll on our bodies, our health. Looking in the mirror, we see a has-been. We remember the good old days, sure that nothing good is ahead. Our goal every day is to just make it, to survive, and to tick off each day that passes on the calendar, just like the prisoner counting off the days of his sentence.

What was supposed to be an overnight stay has gone on indefinitely.

It's just my lot in life…or is it?

6
I CAN GET USED TO THIS...
OR CAN I?

Living in the day-in, day-out drabness of the place to which we've confined ourselves, we embrace a numbness. Though God has sent His angels to minister to us, guided us to the mountain of God for rest, our determination is not to venture out of the place of confinement—even though we've been restored to a reasonable portion of health.

Although no bars or gates are holding us back, we may have created inner signals, fortresses, guard dogs, dragons, moats to keep out the danger and keep ourselves safe, yet these very safeguards may also have served to confine us within. The thought of going out, interacting with others, daring to dream again, daring to hope again is too much to handle. The very idea of again becoming vulnerable to relationship is enough to send us over the edge.

"Nope! Been there, done that, know how that story ends, in heartbreak, and I'm not doing that again" we may think. We may assume that we're too old to start again, or there's "too much water under the bridge."

So we may have numbed ourselves in the companionship of the television and remote control. We may have found comfort in the food we eat; the *evening* cocktail we began to enjoy in the afternoon and now mix with our morning orange juice; the pain pills, prescribed for the pain in our bodies, perhaps now used to deaden the pain in our minds.

What are we making numb? The voice of hope, of possibility, of unfulfilled dreams and purpose, yet pokes us and distantly calls, *"I'm still here!"*

But we continue to numb it, trying to make it go away, attempting to make it stop gnawing at us, bothering us, pestering us to actually make a change.

We tell it to shut up and go away. *"You don't know what you're talking about! It's over for me. I'm coasting through, till one day I close my eyes and breathe my last breath."*

You see, I've gotten used to this life…or have I?

We've made an active and conscious decision to stay floundering in this place. How have we done that? By not agreeing with the voice of God for our lives.

That's a dangerous place to be in, my friend.

We are created beings, and our Manufacturer made within us a God-shaped void that only He can fill.

Scripture tells us that Jesus said, *"Behold, I stand at the door and knock. If anyone hears My voice and opens the door, I will come in to him and dine with him, and he with Me."* (Revelation 3:20 NKJV) However, He cannot come in without our permission.

He stands outside of our cave, watching and weeping as we vainly try to fill up that void with the television, food, or other empty vices, knowing that it's a fruitless endeavor. He knows He's the only One who can fill it—if we would simply open the door.

Let Him in! Do not relegate Him to the porch or the backyard, but let Him in!

If we say that we have no sin, we deceive ourselves, and the truth is not in us. If we confess our sins, He is faithful and just to forgive us our sins and to cleanse us from all unrighteousness.

(1 John 1:8, 9 NKJV).

If, by chance, our weakness of soul has knowingly or unknowingly, willingly or unwillingly, led us into sin, God has made a way of escape, to wipe the slate clean, through confession and forgiveness. We don't have to understand it, but doing it is best. Take advantage of the invaluable free gift by asking for forgiveness of our sins. We have nothing to lose and so much to gain.

What's that sound? It's that knock on the door again. A familiar knock.

I hear a voice, but this time, it's not the voice of the angel...

7
THE AGONIZING QUESTION: "WHAT ARE YOU DOING HERE?"

1 KINGS 19

⁹There he came to a cave, where he spent the night.

But the Lord said to him, "What are you doing here, Elijah?"

The Confrontation

The question is asked by the One who sees all and knows all. Hearing that question stirs up all kinds of emotions and reactions. Nausea results, as the unsettling emotions that have been pushed deep down inside to survive —the anger, the hurt, the fear, the depression, now begin to resurface.

Thoughts that didn't make sense, that don't connect, emerge again. The mind that has been a blur awakens. Words that you have repressed and have not even allowed yourself to speak are liberated. You fear what they will sound like when they pass through your broken heart to your lips—uncensored and uncut—through the polite smile you've learned to wear to cope…to literally survive.

"Will these words come forth like a torrent, like a tidal wave? Will they destroy the hearer? Will God get angry at me for thinking this way and feeling this way?

"What will happen to my stoic demeanor? What will they think of me or say about me when they realize all this hurt was built inside of me?"

On the flip side of this fear may be rage.

This simple question exposes the person you've so neatly confined in this cave. *"What are you doing here?"*

What kind of question is that? Don't You know everything? Didn't You cause this or allow this? Didn't You say You won't put more on us than we can bear? Didn't You say You help those who help themselves? Don't You take the good ones?

If I give voice to why I'm here, will I start weeping? Will I be able to stop the flow? Will the knob even work?

Will my neatly woven façade become unraveled, leaving behind a pile of thread in its place?

What will I do with the shattered pieces of my heart?

What are you doing here, _____? He asked the person by name. *My* name. He's talking to me.

And so you respond.

1 KINGS 19

[10]Elijah replied, "I have zealously served the LORD God Almighty. But the people of Israel have broken their covenant with you, torn down your altars, and killed every one of your prophets. I am the only one left, and now they are trying to kill me, too."

There. You've said it. *"Now You know why I have every good reason to be in this cave. Now, perhaps, You'll leave me alone so I can go on doing what I have to do to survive."*

The Whisper

The result of Elijah's encounter with God is revealed in I Kings 19:11-13.

¹¹"Go out and stand before me on the mountain," the Lord told him. And as Elijah stood there, the Lord passed by, and a mighty windstorm hit the mountain. It was such a terrible blast that the rocks were torn loose, but the Lord was not in the wind. After the wind there was an earthquake, but the Lord was not in the earthquake. ¹²And after the earthquake there was a fire, but the Lord was not in the fire. And after the fire there was the sound of a gentle whisper. ¹³When Elijah heard it, he wrapped his face in his cloak and went out and stood at the entrance of the cave.

And a voice said, "What are you doing here, Elijah?"

You weren't in those storms? I thought they were acts of God?! When I couldn't trust the ground I stood on or what was happening around me, I ducked into this cave. But it's the sound of Your gentle whisper, Your still small voice that draws me… closer… to the door of the cave.

Your Voice…

8
I'M DONE

We may question the catastrophic events that have occurred in our lives. Human nature almost always seems to look for someone to blame. When we can't find a logical reason for the event or if the crisis is larger than life, many fingers point to God.

If God gets named as the culprit (as He so often does), there may be a tendency to recoil into that cave in fear, thinking, "If I can't trust God, who can I trust?"

The Broken Record

As we wrestle with "what happened?" our mind's eye comes up with an explanation that becomes rote—like a broken record that becomes grooved in our minds.

Even after God's display of might in the mountain where He revealed to Elijah that He was not in those catastrophic events of the windstorm, the earthquake or the fire, He again asked Elijah: "Why are you here?"

1 KINGS 19

13bAnd a voice said, "What are you doing here, Elijah?"

14He replied again, "I have zealously served the Lord God Almighty. But the people of Israel have broken their covenant with you, torn down your altars, and killed every one of your prophets. I am the only one left, and now they are trying to kill me, too."

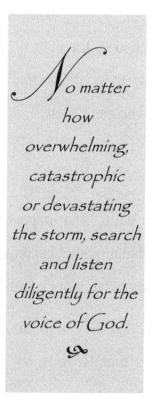

No matter how overwhelming, catastrophic or devastating the storm, search and listen diligently for the voice of God.

Something in Elijah made him respond ever so little to the still, small voice of God, enough to move him out of the depths of the cave, at least to the doorway.

But even in Elijah's movement, his recording was "broken"—repeated word for word as it was *before* the display of God.

Do you remember the old vinyl records? I remember when my albums would sometimes get broken or scratched, and when the needle would get to that particular spot, it would play and replay that part over and over again, until I would have to advance it manually past that point.

Or, I would try putting a coin on the tone arm, so with the aid of that slight bit of extra weight, the needle would flow right through that point, and the music would play again, without interruption.

The Voice of God can be just the weight that's needed for us to advance past the brokenness of our recording.

What's in that Voice? Comfort, truth, reason, understanding, focus, direction, peace, soothing, empowerment.

Surrendering to the Voice of God

Elijah was at a *perfect location* within himself. He had come to the end of himself, to the end of his capabilities, to the end of his strength, to the end of his trust in his fellow man—even to a despairing of his own life.

"How can you possibly say this is a perfect location?"

This is the place of surrender.

Surrender can be that coin on the handle of the record player of your life, surrendering to that power greater than yourself. Surrendering to the super on top of your natural can provide the needed weight to glide over and pass through this experience in your life.

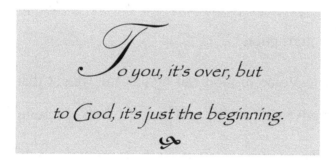

To you, it's over, but to God, it's just the beginning.

Coming out of the cave can be the exciting beginning of a whole new life, lived in a whole new way with a whole new perspective!

With God, all things are possible to them who believe.

When your back is up against the wall, throw your hands up in surrender—not to the circumstance, but to God!

His voice, His still calm voice, has the capability to move mountains.

What's in that voice? Creative power and authority. Will you surrender to that voice? What do you have to lose? There's so much more you can gain.

Hear God's voice guide you past the broken scratch in the recording of your life and seek His direction to your next step...

9

ELEVATOR SHOES

1 KINGS 19

¹⁵Then the Lord told him, "Go back the same way you came, and travel to the wilderness of Damascus."

Go back the same way I came?! Through the wilderness?! I'm trying my hardest NOT to go back again!

Are there people who, if you never had to see them again, even that would be too soon? Are there places from which you have made a break that you vowed you would never return to again?

God, in His infinite wisdom, knows that sometimes before we can effectively go forward, some things behind us may need to be revisited. Just the thought, the very suggestion of going back may bring great emotional upheaval. Are we afraid? Angry? Resentful? Unforgiving? Is there pain? Unseen trauma? Is that place a wilderness? Indeed, a place where dreams were stifled, hope deferred, where more were against you than for you…or so it seemed? Did it seem like you'd never get out of that wilderness and never get past that place of isolation?

Perhaps you experienced depression, rejection, abandonment, heartbreak, loneliness. Just the memory of that location evokes nausea.

You've guarded your heart in this area, perhaps even built a fortress. Yet God says, "Go back!"

You may have been instructed to go back the same way, but you won't go back the same way...the same way you were before. This time, you'll be equipped with 'elevator shoes'.

Elevator shoes. Seeing circumstances from a higher place through the eyes of God. New wisdom, new insight, new power. *"I'm not that same person I was before. You can't define me because I already know I'm loved by my Father. You can't hurt me because the Father is watching, and you don't want to mess with Him!"*

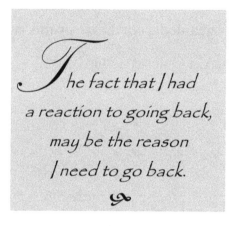

The fact that I had a reaction to going back, may be the reason I need to go back.

I may not need to physically return, but that place may need to be revisited in my mind. Unfinished business remains back there. Holes or blockages, a limp in my stride, an impediment in my speech, a shadow over my vision, a blockage to my flow of love are perhaps a part of "back there." Maybe a release needs to take place. Some illumination or some revelation in places of darkness needs to emerge. Some chains may need to be broken.

Taking this journey in our own timing, strength and volition is not recommended. Rather, the recommendation is that God does the leading. He knows the right time and space. He knows when the conditions are exactly right. He will orchestrate things so perfectly that you'll know that had to have been the hand of God.

The Wilderness

A *wilderness* is defined as:

1) "A tract or region uncultivated and uninhabited by human beings. An area essentially undisturbed by human activity"

2) "An empty or pathless area or region"

3) "A part of a garden devoted to wild growth"

4) "Obsolete"

5) "A confusing multitude or mass"

6) "A bewildering situation"

7) "A position of disfavor"

Although the wilderness may be a difficult place to inhabit, wearing 'elevator shoes' inspires an experience that will cause you to walk back into that wilderness from an elevated position—a place directed by God in His Spirit and in His timing.

Elevator shoes are constructed with the height enhancement on the *inside*, hidden from observers. Likewise, you may look the same on the outside, but the elevated component of God on the inside of you will cause you to now be able to journey through this place from an elevated location and perspective.

A Lift for the Journey

Perhaps counseling is needed to help you deal with the past. A Christian counselor may be God's tool to help you deal with the unfinished or unresolved issues. That journey can bring understanding and clarity, prompt amends to be made, and healing to take place.

ISAIAH 6 (KJV)

[1]In the year that king Uzziah died I saw also the Lord sitting upon a throne, high and lifted up, and his train filled the temple.

[2] Above it stood the seraphims: each one had six wings; with twain he covered his face, and with twain he covered his feet, and with twain he did fly.

[3] And one cried unto another, and said, Holy, holy, holy, is the Lord of hosts: the whole earth is full of his glory.

[4] And the posts of the door moved at the voice of him that cried, and the house was filled with smoke.

[5] Then said I, Woe is me! for I am undone; because I am a man of unclean lips, and I dwell in the midst of a people of unclean lips: for mine eyes have seen the King, the Lord of hosts.

[6] Then flew one of the seraphims unto me, having a live coal in his hand, which he had taken with the tongs from off the altar:

[7] And he laid it upon my mouth, and said, Lo, this hath touched thy lips; and thine iniquity is taken away, and thy sin purged.

Isaiah 6:1 (KJV) says, *"...I also saw the LORD sitting upon a throne, high and lifted up, and his train filled the temple."*

From the elevated place, we can see with more clarity the largeness and the vastness of the majesty of God, get a better look at ourselves in the light of His presence, and receive purification to become all that we need to be.

ॐ

Layers may need to be addressed. We will see ourselves differently and realize where we may have played a part in the problem.

When we're willing to face the pain of the past, deliverance can occur, and breakthrough will come. Healing manifestation will come, and inner elevation will take place, making the outward journey possible.

God will help, lead and guide. He will provide you with divine connections for that portion of your journey.

It's very important not to become captivated by or attached to the person or persons whom God *uses* to aid you through that portion of the journey. Hold them loosely. That person is not God or your savior. The person has been a vessel available to God to assist you in your season. Don't expect the person to be your all-in-all. That individual is human and may disappoint you. Those God uses in your life do not have the capacity to be your heavenly Father!

Don't worry, when their season in your life is over, that does not mean something is wrong with you or them. You are not a reject. See that their season is up, and God has more ahead for you! They are not your last chance!

Your identity comes from your relationship with GOD! So walk on...

10
THAT'S NOT WHAT I
ASKED FOR!

Elijah asked to die, but God says, "Live." You say, *"I can't,"* but God says, "You will."

Sometimes the thought of moving forward is overwhelming, you can't see your way, and you've tried everything you know to do. You can't see any possible way that a positive outcome can be reached. But it can! *"...with God all things are possible"* (Matthew 19:26 KJV).

That voice, which works both ways, is God's creative power. It can quiet the storm and subdue the enemy. It's a two-edged sword dividing asunder the sword and the spirit, bone and marrow. His sword cuts both ways.

You shall not die but live to declare the works of the Lord!

Going down for the last count? GOOD! That's right where God's count begins. Celebrate!

God's Word is like unquenchable fire! It breaks the bars of brass and iron, creates new ground, goes before you, does not return void, but accomplishes everything it has been sent out to do.

His Word declares a new game plan.

Declare is defined as:

1)   To make known formally, officially, explicitly

2)   To make evident

3)   To state emphatically

4)   To make payable

5)   To avow

Can words do all that? Yes, they can! They declare God's authority in your situation. God said it; that settles it. Now you say it too.

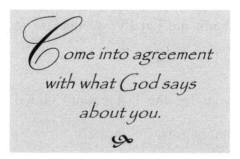

Come into agreement with what God says about you.

You may say it timidly at first, but just say it. You may say it shaking in fear, but say it. You may say it with just a little bit of faith, but say it! You may say it through tears and clenched teeth, but SAY IT!

SAY IT over and over and over until the sound inside goes from a whisper to a ROAR. Say it until the outside noise is drowned out and diminished. Say it, until you BELIEVE IT. SAY IT, AND WALK! SAY IT, AND WALK!

Let the redeemed of the Lord say so! It's as much of a reminder to ourselves as it is to those around us.

I AM REDEEMED! God has redeemed me. What does *redeemed* mean?

- "To buy back"
- "To get or win back"
- "To free from what distresses or harms"
- "To extricate from or help to overcome something detrimental"
- "To release from blame or debt"
- "To free from the consequences of sin"

- "To change for the better"

- "To repair"

- "To restore"

- "To make worthwhile"

No matter what it looks like, on the strength of this new declaration and on the strength of who He is in me and who I am because of Him, I'm coming out of the cave....

11
It's Bright Out There

Spending any amount of time in darkness forces our eyes to make an adjustment. In the process called "dark adaptation," the eye makes multiple modifications to be able to see in low lighting conditions.

Spending time in the cave may also cause dark adaptation in our vision or view of ourselves, our circumstances and others, by way of our perception and perspective.

In her article, "The Caves of Forgotten Time" by Julie Beck, the senior associate editor at *The Atlantic,* the author describes the experiences of two "spelunkers" who lost track of entire weeks as part of an experiment on the effects of isolation in caves in the French Alps near Nice.

Josie Laures spent 88 days, coming out of her cave on March 12, 1965, and she thought or perceived that the date was actually February 25, 1965. Antoine Senni spent 126 days in a cave, emerging on April 5, 1965, thinking and perceiving that the actual date was February 4, 1965.

The two spelunkers (those who explore and/or study caves) had been separated from each other, and researchers tracked their sleeping and eating habits, as well as memory and vital signs. The researchers did not give the spelunkers any clues about how time was passing on the surface. Without any cues from sunlight or clocks, Laures' and Senni's sleep schedules became unpredictable. Senni sometimes nodded off for 30 hours at a time and woke up believing he had only taken a short nap.

Researchers have discovered that people often slip into 48-hour sleep cycles when isolated from their environment. Some studies on the effects of isolation reveal changes in sleep cycles, increased levels of anxiety, hallucinations, and a decline in mental performance.

The article notes that speleologist Michel Siffre also spent six months in a cave near Del Rio, Texas. He reportedly was so lonely that he attempted to catch a mouse to keep as a pet, but aimed poorly, crushing it instead. Laures also turned to

64

rodents for friendship during her time in the cave, which ended up as her sole companions during her three-month ordeal.

"When they emerged from the caves, wearing dark goggles to spare their cave-accustomed eyes from the sunlight reflecting on the alpine snow, they had lost weeks of time, by their own reckoning."

Could our "cave" experiences affect our *perception* ("physical sensations interpreted in the light of experience.") in the same way?

In light of his experience of fear, loneliness, hopelessness, weariness, depression, despair, isolation, Elijah sought refuge in the cave. What he had *perceived* became his *perspective*.

Perspective is defined as "the interrelation in which a subject or its parts are mentally viewed; a point of view."

Elijah's perspective, his point of view, became based on the darkness all around him.

We find that the place into which we've ducked for safety becomes a place where darkness consumes and engulfs us—not only outwardly but also inwardly. It's nearly impossible to emerge from this type of cave without some flicker of light, of hope—without a helping hand or a trustworthy guide to bring us out.

> *God is exactly the One who can lovingly bring us out of that place – from darkness to light.*
> ❧

God beckoned for Elijah to come out of the cave into the light.

Like the spelunkers who lived in a cave in the name of research, when we come out of our cave, we may need to wear 'shades' while our eyes adjust to the light into which we are stepping. Studies show that adapting to light occurs much more quickly than "dark adaptation."

To what light are we adjusting? The Light of God's Truth!

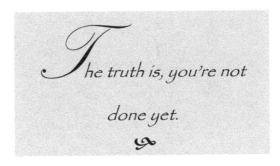

The truth is, you're not done yet.

The truth is you were created for better than this.

The truth is you were created with an innate purpose: God's purpose.

JOHN 1

[1]In the beginning the Word already existed. The Word was with God, and the Word was God.

[2]He existed in the beginning with God.

[3]God created everything through him, and nothing was created except through him.

[4]The Word gave life to everything that was created, and his life brought light to everyone.

[5]The light shines in the darkness, and the darkness can never extinguish it.

Scripture says that the darkness can never extinguish the light.

> *Neither the darkness of the circumstance nor the darkness of the cave can extinguish the light of purpose.*
> ℘

The purpose of shades is to tone down and reduce the glare. The Light, which may be strange, foreign to the eyes or perception at first, can be quite a contrast to the cave experience. But as time goes on, the light becomes more pleasing to the eyes and even adds a perspective and a point of view you enjoy!

In the light you will begin to see certain perceptions, that were once embraced and welcomed in the dark places, may lose their desirability in the light. They will be replaced by a passionate pursuit of your purpose in life.

The cave experience tried to extinguish the light, but quenching that light was impossible. Jeremiah describes this sensation in Jeremiah 20:9 as a "fire in his bones!"

JEREMIAH 20

⁹But if I say I'll never mention the Lord
    or speak in his name,
his word burns in my heart like a fire.
    It's like a fire in my bones!
I am worn out trying to hold it in! I can't do it!

The light of purpose gnaws and persists against all odds and obstacles.

The brightness of His truth brings *clarity* —"the quality or state of being clear." It adds *focus* —"a state or condition permitting clear perception or understanding, direction." His Word says His mercies are new every morning (Lamentations 3:22, 23). The steps of a good man are ordered (Psalm 37:23). Trust in the Lord (Proverbs 3:5). I am with you always, even to the end of the age (Matthew 28:20).

So take off your shades and behold! Step into the brightness of His glory!

12
KING ME

Living a Life Superimposed by the King

Superimpose is defined as "to place or lay over or above something."

Perhaps you've played the game of checkers. The checkers are in array on the checkerboard, with each opponent moving his checkers across the board, and under the right circumstances, has the authority to confront and overtake an opponent's checker. If the player is able to skillfully maneuver his checker against all opposition to the opposite side of the board and reach the final row, he then has earned the opportunity to cry out the phrase, *"King me!"*

That's when your opponent must take one of the checkers you may have lost earlier in the game and place it on top of that checker. Doing so acknowledges that checker as a king with more authority.

Becoming a king gives the checker much more power and ability in the game than it originally had before it was superimposed.

Do I Have What It Takes?

Matthew 25 (MSG)

14-18 "It's also like a man going off on an extended trip. He called his servants together and delegated responsibilities. To one he gave five thousand dollars, to another two thousand, to a third one thousand, depending on their abilities. Then he left. Right off, the first servant went to work and doubled his master's investment. The second did the same. But the man with the single thousand dug a hole and carefully buried his master's money.

19-21 "After a long absence, the master of those three servants came back and settled up with them. The one given five thousand dollars showed him how he had doubled his investment. His master commended him: 'Good work! You did your job well. From now on be my partner.'

22-23 "The servant with the two thousand showed how he also had doubled his master's investment. His master commended him: 'Good work! You did your job well. From now on be my partner.'

24-25"The servant given one thousand said, 'Master, I know you have high standards and hate careless ways, that you demand the best and make no allowances for error. I was afraid I might disappoint you, so I found a good hiding place and secured your money. Here it is, safe and sound down to the last cent.'

26-27"The master was furious. 'That's a terrible way to live! It's criminal to live cautiously like that! If you knew I was after the best, why did you do less than the least? The least you could have done would have been to invest the sum with the bankers, where at least I would have gotten a little interest.

28-30"'Take the thousand and give it to the one who risked the most. And get rid of this "play-it-safe" who won't go out on a limb. Throw him out into utter darkness.'

In The Message translation, Matthew 25 tells a parable or a story of a man who delegated responsibilities to three servants. He gave each man $5,000, $2,000 or $1,000 according to their abilities. The servants given $5,000 and $2,000 doubled their investment, and their master was very pleased. The third hid his $1,000.

This third servant knew he was being given a gift, but he was afraid to mismanage it and disappoint the master, so he found a good "hiding place" and "secured" the money, returning it to the master exactly as it had been given to him.

The way he managed the gift displeased the master who became furious, exclaiming, "That's a terrible way to live! It's criminal to live cautiously like that! If you knew I was after the best, why did you do the least? At the very least, you could have invested it with the bankers and gained some interest! Give it to someone who will do something with it. Get rid of this "play-it-safe" servant who won't go out on a limb."

The man who played it safe infuriated the master. Why did he play it safe and not use the talent or gift?

- Fear
- Comparison with others
- Lowly mindset

These reasons are some of the very reasons why Elijah went into the cave and hid himself. He knew he had God's power and had great talents, yet he didn't feel that who he was could be any match for what was against him. He was essentially afraid he wasn't enough and afraid to disappoint. Even as he came out of the cave, he still probably didn't feel a change inwardly about his abilities nor outwardly concerning his circumstances.

Yet under the unction of the voice of God, he took a step…and then another…and then another.

In taking these steps of obedience, we step out on faith, knowing we can no longer stay where we were, but not quite sure where we're going or how we're getting there. What we do know is that we've stepped out in response to the voice of the King. When we do that, we can cry, "King me!" and we can live and move forward with our lives superimposed by the King.

Suddenly the gifting and abilities we were given become amplified and super-charged. Where we once stuttered, we find ourselves speaking boldly. Where we once limped, we find ourselves bounding. Where we were once shy, we find ourselves confident. Why? Because we've been "kinged"; our life has been superimposed by the Master. Where we were once floundering, we find our life has great purpose and direction.

And so, we step out on faith—faith in the King who has taken up residence in us and on us. As we say yes, He then moves through us. We're no longer playing it safe. We're no longer hiding. Our lives will be fruitful, and God will be pleased with the interest that our life now bears, are according to the abilities He has given to us.

Our gifts and fruit are not to be compared with anyone else's. The fruit we bear is according to the ability and the investment that God has placed within us. The only thing we are to compare ourselves to is the Word of God which we have been given.

That's a hard one, but the sooner we understand this truth, we can get on with the purpose of living a life focused and superimposed by God.

"King Me"—Setting Up Divine Order

1 KINGS 19

¹⁵Then the Lord told him, "Go back the same way you came, and travel to the wilderness of Damascus. When you arrive there, anoint Hazael to be king of Aram. ¹⁶Then anoint Jehu grandson of Nimshito be king of Israel, and anoint Elisha son of Shaphat from the town of Abel-meholah to replace you as my prophet. ¹⁷Anyone who escapes from Hazael will be killed by Jehu, and those who escape Jehu will be killed by Elisha! ¹⁸Yet I will preserve 7,000 others in Israel who have never bowed down to Baal or kissed him!"

Now that we've been "Kinged," we can get on with the business of kingdom building. Elijah was instructed to go to a certain location to anoint and position two particular kings and one particular prophet. Each person had a particular purpose to fulfill for the glory of God; these purposes were intertwined with and dependent upon one another. And, as an assurance to

Elijah, who had originally felt as though he was the only one left, God let him know that He was preserving 7,000 others in Israel who had never bowed down to or agreed with evil.

We are not alone. We may be inclined to look around us and see that 'everyone else' is doing fine and 'nobody else' is going through what we're going through. That is not the case. We have no idea what others are experiencing. They may deal with it more privately and discreetly, but many are going through something.

> *God cares about regions and He cares about people. We have no idea the scope of influence and realms that our seemingly small acts of obedience influence.*

God is looking for people who will hear Him, do exactly what He says, and help with setting up and fulfilling divine order in the earth.

Will you be one?

13
THE OVERFLOW—WHEN OUR INSUFFICIENCY BECOMES OVERFLOW

The biblical story of Elijah speaks of the anointing. *Anointing* is defined as follows:

- "To spread over, to anoint with oil"
- "To anoint anyone as a sacred rite in his inauguration and consecration to an office as a priest, king"
- "Appointed to a specific task by God"
- "To spread out, to expand, to measure"
- "To appoint, or qualify for a special dignity, function or privilege"

The *anointing* can also be defined as "the overflow of Christ in your life." This overflow is increased by spending time in His presence. It's an endowment of Himself on our life.

In his article "7 Things the Anointing Will Do For You," Benny Hinn writes the following:

"The anointing is the power to serve God. Throughout history, God has placed His anointing on people just like you and me whom He's used to do mighty things. When the anointing—the overflow of Christ—comes on your life, it gives you the power to change lives and influence nations."

When the anointing of God comes on our life, it's meant to touch, to consume, to overflow. It's a loving gift for us that is meant to be shared. The anointing is a continuous gift that keeps on giving. It's receiving the charge.

Imagine being given an assignment, then being handed a box with absolutely all the tools needed to accomplish that assignment. That toolbox is lavish and contains more than enough. It's dripping. It spreads. And its flow can only be stopped by us in fear, doubt, or unbelief.

The anointing is sent for the purpose of accomplishing God's perfect will in the earth among His people. It is a rejuvenating force, reviving, restoring health and strength. Its overflow affects those around us. Its assignment carries out the particular purpose and plan of God in the earth, given by His infinite wisdom, grace, foresight and insight.

The anointing causes our insufficiency to be overtaken by overflow for the task. It's God's stamping and qualifying those whom He's called to fulfill His divine purpose.

- It's seasonal.
- It's purposeful.
- It's intentional.
- It's given to be given.
- It's got an assignment and a destination.
- It's to be enjoyed.

Seek to be anointed to overflowing to carry out God's plan.

14
MY SUCCESSOR—
MULTIPLICATION AND
DUPLICATION

1 KINGS 19

¹⁶Then anoint Jehu grandson of Nimshi to be king of Israel, and anoint Elisha son of Shaphat from the town of Abel-meholah to replace you as my prophet. ¹⁹So Elijah went and found Elisha son of Shaphat plowing a field. There were twelve teams of oxen in the field, and Elisha was plowing with the twelfth team. Elijah went over to him and threw his cloak across his shoulders and then walked away.

We were designed to reproduce. Even in the beginning of time, God created the fruit tree to continually yield fruit after its kind.

Seeds were placed inside of us that were meant to impact the world.

Although we may not see our greatness or where we connect, a deposit has been made into us that was meant, through proper development, to break forth with purpose.

How can we determine what to do with it?

How can we determine where to share it?

As we continue to develop in hearing the voice of God by the prompting of His Spirit, we clarify our destination, finding it not to be a location, but the purpose and plan of God.

Elijah was specifically led to Elisha.

2 KINGS 2

⁹When they came to the other side, Elijah said to Elisha, "Tell me what I can do for you before I am taken away."

And Elisha replied, "Please let me inherit a double share of your spirit and become your successor."

Giving to the underprivileged is admirable. Helping the poor is always good. But giving to someone who already shows signs of greatness is something that perhaps God may shine on as well.

That person has been equipped to take your seeds, your contribution, and to carry them to the next level for a greater harvest—to bring forth interest or to add double—even to increase exponentially. The best guidance on how to share them comes from the Lord.

The Seed

Scatter the seed—write a book, blog, generate a YouTube video, develop media, teach a class, be a mentor.

Perhaps you lost a loved one in a way that seemed premature. Perhaps that person left before he or she was able to pass on his or her gifts. Maybe you are called to bring forth the vehicle to reproduce the seed in that person's honor. The possibilities are endless!

What a way to turn tragedy into triumph!!

Our seed, our gift, is not ours to hoard. It was given to us for a purpose—to affect the lives of others and to impact the kingdom of God.

There are sole ingredients that are meant to mix with other ingredients under particular circumstances to produce very spectacular results. ❧

What we may deem as insignificant may be exactly the part that's missing in the whole!

Now that we've come out of the cave, stepping beyond our feelings, gaining new perspective, and following the voice of God, we are ready for the duplication and multiplication to take place.

The Mantle

A *mantle* in itself is simply "a cloak"—an article of clothing worn by many people in Bible times. What made the difference was who was wearing that cloak. In the case of Elijah and Elisha, the mantle represented God's anointing and spiritual authority.

Greater Works

John 14:12 (KJV), *"Verily, verily I say unto you, He that believeth on me, the works that I do shall he do also; and greater works than these shall he do; because I go unto my Father."*

As believers, we have been given a mantle, and the mantle is what we will pass on to others.

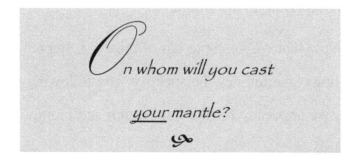

On whom will you cast your mantle?

15
IT'S NOT OVER TILL GOD SAYS SO

When we embark on a mission to do a good work, God's work, to fulfill the purpose and passion that it seems we are born to accomplish, how lovely it would be if the path would be smooth sailing! However, that path may not be uneventful and effortless.

The road to anything great is fraught with challenges.

Challenges, obstacles, opposition—as unpleasant as they may be—reveal what's in us.

From where did Elijah receive his challenges, obstacles and opposition? Examining the traits of Jezebel and Ahab may shed some light on the challenges, obstacles and opposition we face and how to overcome them.

In this biblical account, Jezebel is a very aggressive, hateful, murderous woman, who is hungry for power and dominance. She had no fear of the Lord or regard for man. She hated God and His prophets, and hated truth.

Ahab possessed some fear and respect for the Lord, but his greed overpowered that fear. He aligned his weakness and passivity with a partner who would get things done by any means necessary. Aligning with evil made him evil by association—even though he may not have actually executed the malevolent deeds.

Both Ahab and Jezebel were sworn enemies of those who stood for God and who told the truth. They were irrevocably against the Word of God.

Jezebel vowed to do away with Elijah. She made that oath her sole purpose, top priority and focus. She was a force to be reckoned with. As such, her power may have been a challenge for Elijah, but certainly was not a match for God.

What help did God offer Elijah in his time of distress? What help does He offer us? His unlimited help is made available through praying, reading and speaking His Word, and being in His presence.

Help. The Bible tells us that God is a very present help in the time of trouble (Psalm 46:1). He girds us up, sends His Word, sends His angels; everything is at His disposal.

Wisdom. God gives us of His own wisdom on how to deal with the situation in which we find ourselves.

Knowledge. God grants us knowledge of what we are dealing with and what we need.

Discerning of Spirits. God shows us the type of spirit we are dealing with, beyond face value.

Growth. God makes us strong for the battle.

Know your God. Know your enemy and his tactics. Cover your weak spots. Listen to what's being said. Ask yourself, "Whose voice am I hearing?" Remember, we overcome by the blood of the Lamb and the Word of our testimony (Revelation 12:11).

If we are not careful, we will take on the character of Jezebel to fight Jezebel. What's the true test? Proverbs 3:5, 6 (KKJV), *"Trust in the LORD with all your heart and lean not to your own understanding. In all your ways acknowledge Him, and He will direct your path."* If I'm trusting God, then I'm not forcing outcomes.

Ask yourself the following questions:

"Am I looking to Him or to me?"

"Do I want to save face and be thought admirable, or do I want God's will to be done?" In this trial, our motives are revealed.

"To what lengths am I willing to go to get my way?" Is it my way or the highway, or is it *"...nevertheless not my will, but thine, be done"* (Luke 22:42).

"Is what I want or what I'm doing for His glory or my own?" Am I doing this task for some type of split—a 50/50, 70/30, 80/20—or 100 percent for Him?

"Is He Lord *of* all or Lord *at* all? Get in alignment with God, and let him deal with that spirit and make sure an egotistical spirit is not in you. Check your EGO; ask yourself, "Am I **E**asing **G**od **O**ut?"

"Do I submit to a reign of terror or bow to the reign of God?"

"Will I humble myself for righteousness' sake or proudly insist on being right and having the last word?"

"Do I wear a mask to look good or unmask to be pure?

"Will I manipulate and control, or allow God to be God in my life?"

"When my feelings are confronted with truth, which will I choose?" Deuteronomy 30:19 (KJV) says, *"...I have set before you life and death...therefore choose life...."* that you and your descendants may live, trusting Him when you cannot see the outcome. God's will is life; choose life.

Make some promises:

- "I will be willing to look at myself."
- "I will humble myself."
- "I will stay before God to keep my heart and motives pure."
- "I will repent and keep moving forward."
- "I will give my shame and guilt to God."
- "I will recognize that the battle is Light versus darkness."

When you get to that next location, your strength and supply comes for that leg of the journey. No matter how you feel, keep going! God will supply all your needs (Philippians 4:19)!

16
THE FLIPPED SCRIPT

"Fret not thyself because of evildoers, neither be thou envious against the workers of iniquity. For they shall soon be cut down like the grass, and wither as the green herb" (Psalm 37:1 KJV).

As we step out of the cave and into our purpose, we find we have little time to think about what the adversary is doing because we're walking in the pathway we have been designed to walk. We find our fear is melting and our doubts are fading, as the steps of faith become a reality before us.

Where were Elijah's adversaries?

1 KINGS 22

³⁷So the king [Ahab] died, and his body was taken to Samaria and buried there. ³⁸Then his chariot was washed beside the pool of Samaria, and dogs came and licked his blood at the place where the prostitutes bathed, just as the Lord had promised.

³⁹The rest of the events in Ahab's reign and everything he did, including the story of the ivory palace and the towns he built, are recorded in *The Book of the History of the*

Kings of Israel. ⁴⁰So Ahab died, and his son Ahaziah became the next king.

³⁰When Jezebel, the queen mother, heard that Jehu had come to Jezreel, she painted her eyelids and fixed her hair and sat at a window. ³¹When Jehu entered the gate of the palace, she shouted at him, "Have you come in peace, you murderer? You're just like Zimri, who murdered his master!"

³²Jehu looked up and saw her at the window and shouted, "Who is on my side?" And two or three eunuchs looked out at him. ³³"Throw her down!" Jehu yelled. So they threw her out the window, and her blood spattered against the wall and on the horses. And Jehu trampled her body under his horses' hooves.

³⁴Then Jehu went into the palace and ate and drank. Afterward he said, "Someone go and bury this cursed woman, for she is the daughter of a king." ³⁵But when they went out to bury her, they found only her skull, her feet, and her hands.

³⁶When they returned and told Jehu, he stated, "This fulfills the message from the Lord, which he spoke through his servant Elijah from Tishbe: 'At the plot of land in Jezreel, dogs will eat Jezebel's body. ³⁷Her remains will be scattered like dung on the plot of land in Jezreel, so that no one will be able to recognize her.'"

The evil king and queen died separately; as prophesied, the dogs ate their flesh and licked their blood.

Adversaries are sent to halt forward progression. Take this journey step by step, following God, walking by faith. Those old voices may pop up from time to time. Familiar voices, yet operating through different faces.

What voices tried to stop Elijah?

Ahab—someone who sees your success as an interruption to theirs. Some people feel that the only way they can succeed is by stepping on another's neck.

"Ahabs" may throw roadblocks in your path, hurl accusations or innuendos your way, or try to delay you in any way possible. Strive to move forward with the goal ever before you, knowing that this is God's plan and your destiny. Intend to finish well.

Keep declaring the light and truth of His Word:

- "I will overcome by the blood of the Lamb and the Word of my testimony."
- "I will not fret because of evildoers; neither will I be envious of workers of iniquity. I realize they will soon be cut down as the grass and wither as the green herb."

- "No weapon formed against me shall prosper, and every tongue that rises against me in the judgment will be condemned. This is my inheritance in the saints."
- "Many are the afflictions of the righteous, but the Lord will deliver me from them all."

Accusers or Revealers?

People know our faults and our flaws. Some who are there will aid us in our growth, as a part of their ministry of the perfecting of the saints. From these helpers we will humbly receive the words of correction.

Take them to heart, search yourself, allow truth to reign, make the necessary corrections, be grateful for that one who came along and left you better off than you were before.

The accusers, however, are on a mission to destroy you, your future, your credibility, your opportunities. They are ever present to cast a cloud over your mission to dissuade and break connections, to assail your character and your motives, to ascertain your flaws and to make sure others are focused more on that one blemish, than on the beauty of your face, on that one imperfection rather than the journey you've been on to get to that point and the remaining journey yet before you.

Keep going! Keep your eyes focused on the Lord.

What happened to King Ahab? What happened to the Ahabs in your life who bullied you, rejected you, made you the brunt of their jokes, and treated you with undeserved venom? These Ahabs made sure you were on the outside looking in. They told you that you were the least likely person to succeed.

What happened to that person whose job seemingly was to ruin your life; diminish your self-esteem and confidence; and to constantly remind you of your wrongs, mistakes, sins, unworthiness, imminent failure and demise? Their words, deeds, actions or sometimes inactions seemed to put a nail in your coffin and to ruin any chance of your survival or success.

Where are they now? Did their words and actions stop you?

When God got hold of you and you began to move toward your finish line, you became so busy fulfilling His purpose, walking step by step with Him, that those voices and words became more and more dull as you ignored them and became more attuned to God and purpose.

Then you get the report: "They" met with a horrible fate—not that you'd hoped they would. In Ahab's case, the end was tragic. If anything, you had hoped and prayed they would change.

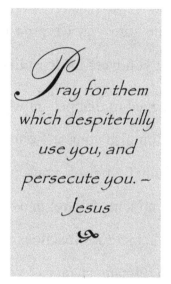

Pray for them which despitefully use you, and persecute you. – Jesus

What about Jezebel? What about the ones who vowed and made it their personal mission to destroy you and everything for which you stood?

Jezebel's threats temporarily shipwrecked Elijah, but she did not permanently stop Elijah from carrying out his purpose. Not until the time of Elijah's successor Elisha did Jezebel meet her horrible end.

Elijah was able to undergo the challenge and overcome his fear by God's empowerment, grace and favor.

17
WELL DONE

2 KINGS 2

¹When the Lord was about to take Elijah up to heaven in a whirlwind, Elijah and Elisha were traveling from Gilgal.

The moment had now come; that is, the moment Elijah waited for.

While in the cave in the throes of the storm, Elijah had begged to die. He could not see his way through, above, below or around the tumultuous circumstances surrounding him. Yet by grace, he was able to come out of the cave, into which he had ducked for safety, and to fulfill his purpose in so many marvelous and miraculous ways!

Not only did he set up kingdoms, and chose and trained a successor, God used him to carry out so much more:

- The past was put in order.
- The present generated great accomplishment.

- The seeds of the future had been planted to continue growth, expansion and flourishing.

God's will for his life was realized; God's purpose for his life was fulfilled.

Elijah could now take joy in that time of inevitability that his life on this great planet was now coming to an end. But this time, the end was bringing fruitfulness with it. This time, instead of hearing, "What are you doing here?" he could now be prepared to hear "Well done."

Isn't that the way we would love to face our end days? Aren't those the words we'd love to hear from the Master?

Come to Jesus while you have time. Plan now to spend your eternity with Him. Leave behind for your family and successors nuggets of faith, truth, and hope, prospering in a way that money cannot buy. Prepare them to sow into the next generation and so on.

Well done, well done.

18
YOUR CHARIOT AWAITS YOU

2 KINGS 2

¹When the Lord was about to take Elijah up to heaven in a whirlwind, Elijah and Elisha were traveling from Gilgal. ²And Elijah said to Elisha, "Stay here, for the Lord has told me to go to Bethel."

But Elisha replied, "As surely as the Lord lives and you yourself live, I will never leave you!" So they went down together to Bethel.

³The group of prophets from Bethel came to Elisha and asked him, "Did you know that the Lord is going to take your master away from you today?"

"Of course I know," Elisha answered. "But be quiet about it."

⁴Then Elijah said to Elisha, "Stay here, for the Lord has told me to go to Jericho."

But Elisha replied again, "As surely as the Lord lives and you yourself live, I will never leave you." So they went on together to Jericho.

⁵Then the group of prophets from Jericho came to Elisha and asked him, "Did you know that the Lord is going to take your master away from you today?"

"Of course I know," Elisha answered. "But be quiet about it."

⁶Then Elijah said to Elisha, "Stay here, for the Lord has told me to go to the Jordan River."

But again Elisha replied, "As surely as the Lord lives and you yourself live, I will never leave you." So they went on together.

⁷Fifty men from the group of prophets also went and watched from a distance as Elijah and Elisha stopped beside the Jordan River. ⁸Then Elijah folded his cloak together and struck the water with it. The river divided, and the two of them went across on dry ground!

⁹When they came to the other side, Elijah said to Elisha, "Tell me what I can do for you before I am taken away."

And Elisha replied, "Please let me inherit a double share of your spirit and become your successor."

¹⁰"You have asked a difficult thing," Elijah replied. "If you see me when I am taken from you, then you will get your request. But if not, then you won't."

¹¹As they were walking along and talking, suddenly a chariot of fire appeared, drawn by horses of fire. It drove between the two men, separating them, and Elijah was carried by a whirlwind into heaven. ¹²Elisha saw it and cried out, "My father! My father! I see the chariots and charioteers of Israel!" And as they disappeared from sight, Elisha tore his clothes in distress.

¹³Elisha picked up Elijah's cloak, which had fallen when he was taken up. Then Elisha returned to the bank of the Jordan River. ¹⁴He struck the water with Elijah's cloak and cried out, "Where is the Lord, the God of Elijah?" Then the river divided, and Elisha went across.

Elijah was able to come out of his C.A.V.E. – his Covering Against the Very Extreme – and followed the voice of God to discover that he was indeed not yet done with his journey. Walking out his journey by following the leadership of God, led him to the successful completion of his journey, out of the cave and into the glory of God.

It is my hope that if you have found yourself, your situation, somewhere in the pages of this book, then you, like Elijah, have decided to come out of your cave with the promise that you are not yet done with your journey!

If you have chosen to follow the steps, I congratulate you. Whether you are like Elijah, finishing up your journey on this earth, or if you are perhaps wrapping up this journey and about to turn the page to start a whole new journey, you did it! I'm glad you didn't give up. I'm glad God brought you through and that He's carrying you in style into your new horizons.

Be proud. Be confident. You've done a marvelous thing. Enjoy the fruit of your labor. You've earned it.

Like Elijah, you've come out of the cave, discovered that you were not done yet, and now are riding into the glory that your obedience has laid before you.

Thank you for allowing me to walk this journey with you. Now off we go, our chariot awaits!

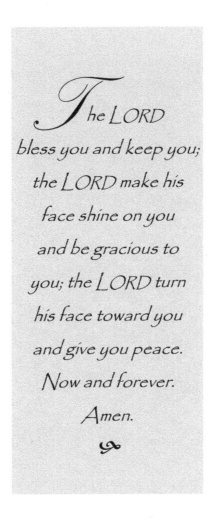

The LORD bless you and keep you; the LORD make his face shine on you and be gracious to you; the LORD turn his face toward you and give you peace. Now and forever. Amen.